LETTERS UNDER ROCK

LETTERS UNDER ROCK

Performance Poetry
Cindy Rinne & Bory Thach

ELYSSAR PRESS
REDLANDS
CALIFORNIA

Copyright © 2019 by Cindy Rinne and Bory Thach
All rights reserved. This book or any portion thereof may not be reproduced or used in any manner whatsoever without the express written permission of the publisher except for the use of brief quotations in a book review.

Printed in the United States of America

First Printing, 2019

ISBN 978-1-7334529-0-8

Elyssar Press
175 Bellevue Ave
Redlands, CA 92373

www.ElyssarPress.com

Cover Illustration Copyright Free from Pixabay by Artsy Bee and A Different Perspective
Cover design by Dan Rinne
Book design and production by Maryse Aoun, www.ElyssarPress.com
Editing by Kelly Dortch and Dan Rinne
Photographs by Edwin Vasquez
Thank you to MOAH in Lancaster, CA for providing the space where the photographs were taken during "The Woven Stories" exhibition curated by Andi Campognone, 2019

For Elena

Introduction
Seasons
Ganesh admires branches reaching towards rebirth

Letters Under Rock

Chapter 1: Night Wanderings
Address/Endless
Hush/Unchanged
Birth/Daybreak
Wilderness/Reunion
Air/Hum

Chapter 2: Orphan with Love Letters
Tension/Regrets
Sage/Psalm
Map/Hand
Womb/Floating
Moon/Spirals

Chapter 3: Shadow River
Halo/Hunters
Witness/Maya
Lack/Grace
Gaze/Cycle

Chapter 4: Karmic Roots
Silken/Earth
Shadow/Lullaby
Ancestors/Dream
Stomp/Cold
Awaken/Moonlight
New/Tomorrow

Chapter 5: Relearn the World
Haunted/Vibrations
Mirage/Kindred
Conscious/Rebirth
Relearn/Balance

Epilogue
Reflection/Another

Introduction

"Letters Under Rock" Poetry Performance collects from many landscapes and faith traditions: Morocco, Ireland, the Sahara, India, Japan, Cambodia, etc. Animism, Angels, Tibetan Buddhism, Hinduism, Desert Mothers, Saints, etc. There are rituals, ghosts, forest spirits, rebirth, mollusk that tells a story, dragon, heron, swan. This story reaches across time and space told in love letters left under a rock of an orphan Wanderer and a Nomad.

How the performance and story came to be:

Cindy

Conchi Sanford, curator and artist, asked me to be in an exhibit of collaborations at The Progress Gallery, Pomona, CA. I wanted to create an installation of my costume art. My collaboration began by asking Bory Thach to write a poem in response to the imagery on one of my garments. He agreed and I stitched his poem "Seasons" to silk for the back of the dress.

Performance was another possibility for this collaborative exhibit. I took some drama workshops with the idea of moving in the direction of performance poetry. Conchi suggested that my costumes in the exhibit be worn. Next, I asked Bory if he would be interested in performing poems wearing a coat I had designed. He said yes. We had two months to create the performance. We started by writing call and response poems. These became letters. The characters of Wanderer and Nomad appeared.

We also attended a poetry performance workshop by Brian Sonia-Wallace which helped us to "see" our performance past being thoughts on paper. Bory and I choreographed movements based on two poems inspired by the costume "Seasons" and the ten poems that begin the book. The performance "Letters Under Rock" was well-received. We were hooked!

Bory and I decided to continue writing letters. It was exciting for me to receive his poems. A narrative of loss and longing between two lovers began to grow, shift, and surprise. I sensed we were getting close to an ending of this aspect of the story. Bory agreed. The Epilogue allowed for transformation and the future.

The evolution of "Letters Under Rock" has expanded into other iterations including: others creating art based on some of the poems; I stitched a 12'x2' tapestry inspired by three poems in the book for "Woven Stories" curated by Andi Campognone at MOAH in Lancaster, CA; I designed and sewed costumes for our poetry performance based on some of the poems. What's next?

Bory

I had been writing poems for some time and wasn't sure if they were parts of each other. But Cindy Rinne asked me to write a response to her fabric art piece, and I agreed because creativity included individual interpretation. Once I completed "Seasons" and Cindy wrote her own poem in conjunction with it, we both knew that this was the beginning of our journey. My character of Nomad had made his appearance alongside Cindy's orphan, the Wanderer.

Our first ten poems took on a performative aspect and that further influenced the way we perceived the entire manuscript. Each additional poem continued the story arc of our protagonists, a tale of two spirit bodies following one another, their souls moving through time and space, connected by true love's eternal power. There are familiar threads, images, and ideas that weave throughout "Letters Under Rock" as well as more unfamiliar and unexpected concepts which span different continents, religious traditions, and cultural practices.

This collaborative work symbolizes mutual respect and admiration between us. The collection "Letters Under Rock" tells the story of life, love, and death as we experience what it means to be human and spiritual beings while also transcending those limitations. Both Cindy and I draw from our own lives, what makes us individually unique as well as those strong beliefs, values, common interests that bring creative minds together.

The book deals with ideas of faith, spirituality, personal histories that answer questions with more unanswered ones. I'm grateful to have worked with such an amazing artist, and I can't think of a better friend than Cindy Rinne. We share each other's philosophies on existence. Her belief in the universe's higher power that guides us toward peace and harmony remains true to me, unchanged even after many mistakes I've made as long as hope is alive. We continue to succeed and live through adversities even after unbearable heartbreak.

Wanderer

Nomad

Seasons

Photo credit by Genevieve Kaplan, Photo taken at the Progress Gallery, Pomona, CA

Give me a piece of blue sky,
I walk through blades of grass.

The eagle's strength surpasses our own;
A freedom we can only hope for.
We cannot deny

The wildness of our hearts.
Old tales, like ancient roads,
Go on forever.

Even if we lose ourselves,
Love will never be forgotten,
As nature always keeps its promises.

The sacred, white elephant dances
As we dream. Our clothes change
Colors with the seasons of loneliness.

Fall withers away into winter,
And the world renews itself in spring.
War flags wave on horseback,

Drum sounds awaken souls roosting
Inside limestone caves alongside
Martins and swallows.

They eclipse the sky in a panic.

I borrow the desert as a thread
From the goddess of love.
It becomes the mantle,

Protecting you from the cold.

The beams of light flow against
Your hair in an elegant pose.
The distance between us disappears

Into beauty and warmth. Abandoning Ourselves,
We embrace and become one
With sky and earth.

*Ganesh admires branches reaching
towards rebirth*

in the desert under Joshua tree shade. a nomad
made of milky way told the story of two lovers,
farhad and shirin, as nutmeg elephants in jeweled blankets
listened to the windswept tale.

a forbidden love is royal and common. a rock carver created–
a petroglyph in stone of the princess before he dug a canal,
a well for desert waters to win permission for marriage
but was told a lie,

shirin had died. his tools as suicide. a band of light—shirin faced
death and joined her blood with his.
red tulips as their perfect love.

Joshua Tree - Photo credit by Cindy Rinne

"Relearn Being in the World" (detail)
Art Piece by Cindy Rinne

LETTERS UNDER ROCK

Cindy and Bory Entrance:
Across from each other.

Cindy WALKS in first and sets up the altar.

Bory WALKS in.

Both SMILE at each other.

Cindy: Nomad, is that you?

Bory: Is it really you, Wanderer?

Cindy: Yes. I've finally found you.

Bory: I've always been with you. In these pages, your letters are all I look forward to.

Chapter 1
Night Wanderings

*A good traveler has no fixed plans
And is not intent on arriving.*
— Lao Tzu

*The night walked down the sky
with the moon in her hand.*
— Frederick L. Knowles

ADDRESS | HUSH | BIRTH | WILDERNESS | AIR

Dear Nomad,

Sound broken by pigeons
On wires singing a sad song in the mists—

I cannot fit through that window anymore.
    The panes melt in the flames.
        The mailbox disappears,
            But the eternal spring gurgles.

No address brings wandering
As the pepper tree sways
In one last whisper.

Dear Wanderer,

Beauty steals the soul—
without a dream to chase,
I walk in search of you.
But we are separated within
form and desire.

Life gives me love.
Seeking truth and hope
I exist only with you
by my side.

Silence is not
    without sound.
    We wait
        to meet again—
                in the four heavens.

Ten thousand miles like falling peach
flowers, their panic standing
between us and the world.

Memories go back and forth,
you come to me when I'm asleep.
The moon reflects the mirror.

We grasp our hands together
As the night wanders, becoming endless.

Dear Nomad,

Blue dawn brightens
Pleiades, icy sun,
And hibiscus like snowflakes
Planted as totem.

Against the drifting fog,
Three guardian trees
Imprint the shrouded mountain.

I vibrate in the unbroken
Starlight as mist,

As angel.

Hush.

Dear Wanderer,

The past comes back, gathering like a flower
Withered wishes. It's amazing how sea,
sky
Share the same color. I watch you fly
Up into that seafloor,

So endlessly wide and eternal.
We reach the flooded sky—
Widespread wings.
Love unchanged. My tears flow back to you.
As burning incense turns to snow,
And lightning bolts dance in our palms.

One yields a lotus
The other a red string.

LETTERS UNDER ROCK

ADDRESS | HUSH | **BIRTH** | WILDERNESS | AIR

Dear Nomad,

It's raining harder. Thunder crashes
longer nights, leaves crunch,
trees bare orphan bones.

In crisp darkness,
clouds clear
the world births
from stars, shivers
as the woman screams
and animals stream around
her split spirit body,

        octopus, spider, and snake.

Embroidered
harvest moon colors
outline the birth pain.
Gold threads
couched for a phoenix
to marry a dragon chasing

        a pearl.

Dear Wanderer,

Night comes with it a comforting silence
as I stare up at the sky of sparkling cities
angel wings on balancing scales.

The lanterns burn the oil
until breaking dawn.
Life and death can be lonely,
scattered,
      broken needles—
                            a tapestry of fate.

When my heart has fallen into an abyss,
your face appears. Am I awake or dreaming?

Out of the firelight, I walk
into the desert wilderness
to meditate. A dream-filled wakefulness,
thoughts run
wild without end or beginning—
I forget to breathe.

A knife carves open memories.

LETTERS UNDER ROCK

ADDRESS | HUSH | BIRTH | **WILDERNESS** | AIR

Dear Nomad,

Native soil
Old roots
Worn stones
Saguaros march
Birds gather
Raven floats
Canyon ash
Hummingbirds
Dead branches
Red hills
Tears swell
Eyes sting

I drink from the well,
swallow ancient
language, earth fire.

Dear Wanderer,

A thousand years or ten thousand,
We'll never forget each other.
Even if the river changes direction,
Eyes like blue waves walk through
My past lives.
Our destiny rotates from age to age.

I read your palm how I read the night sky.
Holding onto a picture of you,
Seeking through this world for your likeness,

Only to find it in a poem—that place where life meets.
We can wait there and watch the sun,
A lovely place to sing.

Winds blow across the three realms,
Heaven and earth separate like
This life and the hereafter.
I write a love letter
Under moonlight
And watch meteors fall.

Every moment in time already printed,
Every reunion and every sunset.
The ink never fades, just as lovers follow
After one another always.

ADDRESS | HUSH | BIRTH | WILDERNESS | **AIR**

Dear Nomad,

Sparse leaf suspends—

falls

Its essence reverberates

Body sways
Souls cluster like a wind chime

The distance promises musk regeneration
together
as the leaf spins

and the ripples fade

Dear Wanderer,

I ask when we can meet again.
The moon,

a blank stare without words.

                      Chants.

If only I could hum   stars

and break the world   begin anew.

Would you   return with it?

Chapter 2
Orphan with Love Letters

*Map the places that live in your memory
Map the voices of the land*
— Adam Loften & Vaughan-Lee

*Celebrate the boundary
Where streams join the sea,
Where body meets infinity.*
— Lorin Roche

TENSION | SAGE | MAP | WOMB | MOON

Dear Nomad,

We both create innermost anima
to cast shadows
to escape the mundane,
to capture light past limitations.

Dawn clutches out of control—

the doll flutters her eyes to sleep,
the mystery book clasps shut,
the lotus pushes through mud.

Reality and make-believe
blur between
reflected lines.

Dear Wanderer,

Forever in a moment—
you are the end of my life.
Only to guard you, I've crossed
the forgotten river and become enemies
with the world.

Holding a line of words,
I'll ask to marry the gods and accompany
you to watch another rising sun.

The changing sea, full of emotion—
makes anything possible.
The altar no longer exists.

Dear Nomad,

I forget to photograph
the skull by the curb

Split in two pieces,
canine teeth not facing
each other to bite

*

Starting at the bottom
tombstones stretch
as arms reach beyond

the tangerine sunset
to a glacial orb

The Sage speaks
for forty years
without saying a word

Patterns of a brain
as lobes vein.
*What is absent
from your grasp?*

Dear Wanderer,

With the cosmos falling apart,
you alone make it beautiful—
perfect things come with regret.

Time goes on—
our story gets rewritten,
                                and we smile

against the harsh words.
Every droplet of our past
brings me back.

For your face has become
a psalm of memory,
never to be forgotten.

TENSION | SAGE | **MAP** | WOMB | MOON

Dear Nomad,

Among lonely fog,

a cormorant perches on driftwood forts,
ghost limbs, in a forest of oak and ash.
I, too, am crimson trees reflected
in brassy waters. Red thread ties
around my trunk. A reflection
of my soul. Every thin branch
cracks in ice. Fire burns
contained by edges of snow above
permafrost below.

Dear Wanderer,

A soul awakens,
an irresistible force
set in motion by the fairy goddess of light
and darkness. Clouds of mist rise
from burning lakes. Treeless mountains
circle the high skies.

Red dust colors the air,
                      life breathes into being.

Fresh blood covers the sea of sand,
giving shape to the formless clay—

              existence and desire
              become flesh.

The beating of wooden drums,
their voices
              travel   along
rivers

and stream   through

valleys beyond.

Stars dwindle

a horizon,
              sunshine
                                  breaks
through

                                        smoke.

Dear Nomad,

Beneath the giant, golden Buddha,

before friends and family,

I heard promises from the womb

that they would love each other

always, take care of me as a yogi.

They met dancing under India

moon. My half-brother shies away

from the attention. Still, smiles

and hugs my mother briefly. Father holds

him close. Looks into her

meditative brown eyes. Rubs her belly. The room fills

with white cotton, laughter, and watermelon juice.

The revelation—I am a girl, soon to dance into the world.

Later, flowers turn brown. Just Mother and I chant.

Promises snuffed out as smoke swirls to the painted ceiling.

Dear Wanderer,

A cluster of stars reveal where we once stood. The room

floating overwhelms us, shades of lavender and magenta,

so beautiful how they blend like dreams inside of dreams.

We kiss to silence the gray static in our ears, hearts

become one under a new sky. The autumn moon,
partially

hidden behind curtains that replace the walls, it expands

in waves with every touch, fading with the midnight air.

I can't see your orphan spirit wandering. We use both

hands to embrace. The whole universe resounds within

Gabriel's Horn. Eyes become full and endless as the sea.

Towers sway in the distance, low hanging power lines

crackle, sparks burn the water, and we fall only to
become

smothered embers.

TENSION | SAGE | MAP | WOMB | **MOON**

Dear Nomad,

Lavender water pulses
between moss rocks

cranial nerves heal
chew, bite, smell
red spine, ribs

Twelve wires strung
in bands of three

strum into elk
skull Antlers strain

under new moon
Hecate, luminous,

walks on roads, ingests

belladonna from corked
glass Sees
the otherworld

perceives this brain's
destiny, a crossroads

Dear Wanderer,

The scorpion skitters across desert
moonlight, sacred sand separates
all the worlds between gods
and creation. Water spirals
with a gentle breeze,
the soul burns

                                      nirvana

flames.

Falling stars cool upon landing.
Seed the earth.
A book without words.
An affectionate shadow, its lasting feeling
awakens to a lyric.

The red lotus becomes a phoenix flower—
ashes bloom to perfect
mortality.
A moth, fearless and living towards death,
throws itself into the sea.

Chapter 3
Shadow River

*Eventually, all things merge into one,
and a river runs through it.
The river was cut by the world's great
flood and runs over rocks
from the basement of time. On some
of the rocks are timeless raindrops.*
— Norman Maclean

*Love is a naked shadow
on a gnarled and naked tree.*
— Langston Hughes

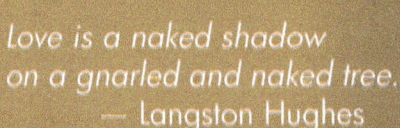

Dear Nomad,

I am the white-lined sphinx moth with brown head and thorax
flight like a hummingbird. My body too large for its wings.
A placid lake performing a moth ritual each morning

before the night travelers sleep. They tell of a face
in a mollusk shell who shares a story. A prayer written
and burned thanks the night for moon and stars
that navigate my path. I bring healing to others

drink
the moon's halo.

At dusk wildflowers speak of seeds blown to the sea.
A young mother battles cancer for years,
reborn.

Her sister lives in the rocks by the ocean,

with her baby—
they sit in the sand and
rock to endless rhythm.

A shadow song:
Safe. Small. Nature is large. I want to feel small again.

HALO | WITNESS | LACK | GAZE

Dear Wanderer,

On moonless nights, hunters awaken
with smoking torches—
the enraged rock bees give chase
after sparks of burning incense

fused into one hallowed shell.
Flowers of disk-shaped honeycombs
pinnate along smooth, silvery bark
like tough feathery crowns.

Beneath drooping evergreen leaves,
robbed of sunlight,
encircled by a canopy of roots—
only to become a sacred Tualang.

Singers chant prayers until dawn while
souls of the dead climb branches
reaching heaven.

Dear Nomad,

Traveler
Stand in the center of the oak tribe,
interconnected trees where roots mirror branches
encircle my feet. Trunks almost hugging,
sun filters golden through green leaves
with yellow edges as season shifts.

Whispers
I turn, place my hand on the rough trunk,
and ask, How are you?

Well, for the most part I am good, answers the oak.
*The Ponderosa pine standing alone nearby
causes some friction through its prickly personality.
Likes to debate the take-over of the forest by squirrels.*

Promises
Duir arrives to discern the poisonous from the safe.
She implores me to follow her to the silver firs.
Drink this tea of rounded pine needles for inflammation.

Tastes like drinking the forest, windblown and expansive.

Ingest to connect with the nature that you are,
she explains.

Next, spider wants to spin a home between my ribs,
transitory and pure.

Dear Wanderer,

Mangrove forests swallow coastlines.
Aerial roots churn stars into galaxies of milk.
The regenerated heavens carry sound
and Earth vibrates. A world above ours,
one cannot see.

My ego tethers me
to this reality. I pray and beg
forgiveness,
                              as the seas mingle with fire.

A bloom of flapping wings, dawn bats
fed on pollen and nectar in ritual
sacrifice. We are children born

from nature,

wading through fields
shimmering
to stay afloat,

apple orchards flowering at dusk.

Dear Nomad,

I.
Eucalyptus stretch and dance
barren ghosts their scent
lingers around the hollow bend.

Leaves gray. I try to forget.

Forgiveness tastes bittersweet
behind the stained, blue door
anchored to earth by angled stone.
Cracks in the patterned tiles engrave
your name.

Eat the skin, but not the seed.

You left. This caused me pain,
but a gain of freedom to believe
all things meant tearing,
like pulling out cacti by their
roots laid bare.

II.
Maple leaves fall in the windblown
spring of autumn. Birth and annihilation
lead me to your footsteps. A single thought
becomes an obsession,
just as invisible scars
never heal.

An endless stream moving in circles.
Joyful sorrows rooted in my bones
only to whisper old songs of impermanence.

I'm waiting between worlds.
With you every word and phrase,
a memory left in verse.

III.
Forgive.
Forgive.
Forget me.

Dear Wanderer,

I.
Fairy lights dance around
storm clouds and ripple
like water. A hypnotic
suggestion.

Rainbow colors with lightning
paints the ground in waves against
an airglow sky.

We say farewell between our lips.

The deep sea shines from inside a dream
of frozen memories. Tombstones scatter
on roadsides like spirit lanterns.
Unforgettable promises marred by
your silhouette.

Eyes as lonely as moonlight.

II.
Listen: The fishing pole captures
a star that dissipates into a meadow
of spring flowers. Solstice sun
paints clouds on spiral sky. Dragonfly
rests on cattails following the compass
of low, harvest moon. Close your eyes
and view snowflake sprites
sprinkled on my hood and shoulders.

III.
Let the sleet kiss you.
The realigning of stars.
I search for morning grace.

Dear Nomad,
[*Tao in the world is like a river flowing home to the sea.*
Lao Tzu]

We gaze in two planes intersecting.
The future a compass, a map
made of soundwaves.
Swan blends into raven faces
opposite directions. The light
of the universe is upon me
daily I walk

and listen to graveyard voices.
Damp tombstones cause my feet
to slip surrounded by forest spirits.
I discover one split with a child's name.

Another aged marker reads between the mosses,
Boatman sails across the sea.

These pillars embrace between thin trunks.
Carved hearts broken among a carpet of oak leaves.
We spill our bones at dawn.

Dear Wanderer,

In a permanent twilight,
ravens eat the flesh of saints.
During harvest season
we navigate by stars and search
for dawn.
An eternity to cultivate my spirit
while I shed tears of ashes over a fallen
world.

Scripture of wisdom echoes.
Knowledge passes through time
as the mind's eye never forgets.
Like silk cloths, stained with frost.
And the lightness of our faces become
discarded. We meet inside a cloudy mirror
that reflects life at first sight.

We fade away
into evergreens, strong and standing
for centuries
among sagebrush valleys.

Chapter 4
Karmic Roots

*How can I hold something
in my hand and hear
a voice halfway around the world?*
—"Madness, Rack, and Honey"
by Mary Ruefle

*The deeper that sorrow carves
into your being,
the more joy you can contain.*
— Kahlil Gibran

SILKEN | SHADOW | ANCESTORS | STOMP | AWAKEN | NEW

[All great and precious things are lonely.
John Steinbeck]

Dear Nomad,

I carry saffron threads from the fields of Suktana
   for trade and think of Amma Sarah of the Desert
in her monastic cell near the Nile, ignored.
   Infinite.

Your far-reaching fingers tie an orange, silken ribbon
   on my left wrist like a bracelet. A marker of when
we were together. Primordial faces exposed. I need more
   time to reveal family secrets. Roots

hidden deep like tamarisk bushes of slender branches
   and gray-green leaves. To a cluster of pink
agapanthus, I depart to hike with difficult footing
   quartz cubes cut, and pine cones

crumble. Before sunset, my demons whisper,
   Jump into the rushing river. I bury them in a crypt.
Lightning divides the North Star. A sudden wall of tears
   whips through my skin of shame. Nothing more I can
do.

Power if I can forget myself.
I transmute into desert flood.

Dear Wanderer,

The earth speaks through us
after hiking up Khao I Dang Mountain.
We stand at the top of a crescent hill,
shaded by the coolness of the mountain's
shadow. Callioped trees
rise toward a sunset sky.
The fields of coconuts,
and bananas fruit on vines as witness.
Cantaloupes sprout into wilderness
unborn.

I imagine myself evergreen
or yellow jubilee, red-flesh twin—
different from usual green melons.
Golden rinds like halos, protective crowns
against sprites and dwarfs living inside hallowed trees.
A crimson sweet taste, my thoughts of departure search
among tall wheat grass and follow water sounds.

EARTH | LULLABY | DREAM | COLD | MOONLIGHT | TOMORROW

[The highest of goodness is like water, for water is excellent in benefitting all things. Lao Tzu]

Dear Nomad,

Yellow butterfly lands on Damask rose.
Sunrise, I enter a higher world.
Absence of shadows. Every thought
brought into silence.
Myths are true.
The kalash filled with water and love
held high in both hands.

Wind swirls the Persian plum tree and stops.
Water disturbed when lifted to the sky
like a gentle rain poured
to the sun's soul. I call
for storms to nourish.
Snow to protect seedlings.
A spirit water strengthens
me with health, abundance, and wisdom.

Huma never touching earth says goodbye.
A song for the essence
fish, deer, horses,
lavender, olives, and grains.
Lands traveled and places
before me. Ballad for those I meet
quenching my thirst.
This chorus douses you.
Imbathed wherever your life cycles emerge.

Dear Wanderer,

The seawater recedes as celestial nymphs and naga serpents drink up surrounding oceans, giving birth to dryland. To tell a story recorded in the depths of clouds, there is no balance without peace. My origins of god-kings, Kambuja warriors that descend from Suvarnabhumi, the Golden Land. A divination between heaven and earth.

A holy destiny slashing its way to victory, every brush stroke draws out an image of you. I chase the setting sun, trying to make the day last while winds sweep through a moonless battleground. Romantic courage from our past lives repays the debt.

Renowned prince implores the gods with the help of Lord Shiva. They grant him a most beautiful bride.

A waking dream like gentle breeze, eyes lonelier than moonlight paints your bones, I cannot reach your essence. The sprouts of blood become flowers beneath our feet.

SILKEN | SHADOW | ANCESTORS | STOMP | AWAKEN | NEW

Dear Nomad,

I lean sideways in front of the cypress mirror and brush
my hair one hundred times as my mother taught me.

Soak this dress with three figs across the bodice
on powder blue cotton, in the oasis, squeezing water

into my mouth. Beyond my reach, the inherited dress floats
through the layers of stacked beings encased in clouds

while light brown rabbits, sensitive and kind, scamper
like gusty winds in four directions. Heavenly and earthly

realms join. Ashen wolf and deer my origin. Date palms
reach, attempting to grab the dress which dodges

like a balloon. I set the brush down, smooth my dress,
and watch rabbits leap in salt grasses. Tell me the truth.

Be my witness.

The dress. The dress. The dress.

Dear Wanderer,

Love deserves an aftertaste

before night fades into the sunrise.
Purple lightning through dark clouds,

sage green sky over dead tree.
An arm-like hand to hold up the Milky Way.
Infinite stars conquer storm
and preside over turmoil. A cloud
of empty ghosts

moves toward the crows. Lacking strength
I see another trembling
kiss by your lips separated by yin and yang.
Break away from the spider's web. Awaken

to truth without intoxication
like tornado over water,

the red afterglow above ionosphere,
I become helpless as drifting

leaves of lavender.
A dreamland I miss and regret

where we borrow happiness...

LETTERS UNDER ROCK

SILKEN | SHADOW | ANCESTORS | **STOMP** | AWAKEN | NEW

Dear Nomad,

Aurora pulsates.
I dream of homes—
purple roofs,
red walls, yellow doors.
Mother zig-zags across indigo sands

      drift
blast
                         spill
    ephemeral
                              flow
  stomp

Vanishes knotted to a silver thread,
carp floats, target-shape golden eyes,
paper scales with open mouth,
collectswindspirit
                      stomp
     jump
           twirl
touchground
                     bend

        kick
bow

Your skin, strokes of flame
not seeing, repeats damaru,
creation/preservation/dissolution
peace beats of tribe

pulltaut
                twistwrist

    spiritenergy
                stomp

Speckled and orange carp
traverseripplelines,
      the shadow passing overhead
           like a phantom ship,
                stitched borealis

LETTERS UNDER ROCK

Dear Wanderer,

Staring into the night
I dream of glittering cities,
floating palaces in the sky

I awaken to eyes burning into mine

only to shed tears
                     over the changing
seasons

The coldest lake,
heartless streams of water
                     travel far beyond our senses

without karmic roots

LETTERS UNDER ROCK

EARTH | LULLABY | DREAM | **COLD** | MOONLIGHT | TOMORROW

Clear and placid mind
watches you from afar

                              magnificent

predestination

Frost melts into words

                              I see poetry

in the flames

Hate and regret disappear
the fall of a dynasty
                an empty desert
                both dazzling and sorrowful

SILKEN | SHADOW | ANCESTORS | STOMP | **AWAKEN** | NEW

Dear Nomad,

ancient limestone cups **memories**
built in this dense place

fossils weep and wings turn **dark**.
An altered environment, a rosy fjord,

        migration **not needed**,
        impermanent.

LETTERS UNDER ROCK

EARTH | LULLABY | DREAM | COLD | **MOONLIGHT** | TOMORROW

Dear Wanderer,

cannot wake from this dream

ignore the sadness,

I burn pen and paper
to write you again.

[Who is the Buddha? The mountains are traveling over the sea. Zen Buddhism]

Dear Nomad,

Between the east and west
pinks of dawn—
          a shooting star

Infinite blue mountains,
color of glass beads—
          a prayer to the sun

Ang Sung Wahe Guru,
the limitless dancing—
          within me

Dear Wanderer,

Time flows by unabated
as the sunset casts
memories.

A temple ridge
traverses thousands of miles—
an ancient pilgrimage.

Beauty intoxicates
youth vanishes
leaving behind an injury.

I'm damaged by your charm.

I don't regret tomorrow
because of you.

Chapter 5
Relearn the World

*In difficult times you should always carry
something beautiful in your mind.*
— Blaise Pascal

*Our greatest glory is not in never failing,
but in rising every time we fall.*
— Confucius

LETTERS UNDER ROCK

Dear Nomad,

How many tomorrows?

Earth mother, my skin splits like textured
flakes of an old oak tree. Sunken eyes.
My hands unknot the webs. I sit cramped
in the corner radiating pyramids.

I mourn the loss
maiden to crone
alone in an ice cave, an entrance
guarded by Garnr.
Fever
chills
encompass me.

> Is this not baptism by thorns?
> You would salve my wounds.
> Instead, I drink tea of holly
> leaves trying to heal.

Where are you?

River runs beyond my stomach.
I wear a death mask. Is Hel,
one-half bones, the other divine
preparing the transition of my soul?

> Seers and shamans will travel
> for my counsel. I will give them
> holly for strength and wisdom.

I need

to see you.

Dear Wanderer,

Born from the Earth, a child of nature
among purity and innocence. Spiritual
happiness. Tranquil love between you
and me. Face paler than snow
with ember eyes.

Why do you seem so familiar?

> I'm in a stream of stars at night,
> reflecting on the waves.
> Delicate lilacs cover your wounds.
> Sharp eyes transform into fire.

Birds, paper the sky, only to leave star
trails. Calm, my mind as passionate
mountains where twilight dawns
into late spring, and time itself
spikes non-linear.

Unable to turn away, I stare, moon-eyed
underwater while a bromeliad emerges
from vibrations of mantras.

You
                take away my sorrow.

*[Love alone is the fountain from which all virtues fall
as drops of sparkling water. Hazrat Inayat Khan]*

Dear Nomad,

        Angel cries out / from a well,
          Come for the water blessing.

She stands knee-deep in holy water / while streaks of diagonal clouds diverge. Water drops plop and echo / as she rises. Crystal eyes reflect / in the filled bowl.

              I approach / in silence,
eyes downcast / and wait to be cleansed. Incense permeates. The angel / chants and prepares / with care. / Blesses thyme flowers, rice, and well water.

           She pours / the sacred
over my head / into the fertile canyons of my body. Sun blinds my drenched eyes. I wake to dry heat / and a Tri Dhatu bracelet on my wrist / to resist disaster.

          I am girdled by granular,
transparent crystals / female divinity like Salacia of the calm and sunlit sea, / once a verdant plain. Our child would be / half human, half fish.

Dear Wanderer,

       Different lives we have / coming and going.
         All return to that river in the sky.

Wisdom flows through prophetic mouths / water
from the Stream of Forgetfulness
cannot wipe away my yearning. / Time
                         goes by.
Each step / not
            a waste. The parting /
sorrow, the bamboo flute speaks a solemn
story / of elegant tears. Against a purple
sky / the hunter with arrow in hand, raises his
bow. / Nothing but a dark and empty outline.

            I stare at the wolf / howl
at the moon / hoping she would be his. He knows
she can never be / yet he cries until dawn
breaking. / The holy reverence, I watch this
haunting ritual.

           A conjuring spell. Dark
clouds / erupt and thunder in startled anticipation. /
Rage-filled sky dissipates
to sunshine peering / through kindred souls.

           I let chaos go / in exchange
for moments / of happiness. Divine plan and purpose /
carry as one. In the end, reach the light on a long road.
Wolf eyes flicker like hot steel as I gaze at the hunter
who recognizes mine as his own.

Dear Nomad,

If I place quartz stones in a stream,
will the sparkle in moonlight
draw you near like salmon longing for home?

Home is within me

Here

Where I find contentment

If I drink forgetfulness from Lethe, will I pass
into new life
as hunter or wolf? Will you know me?

Nowhere

Where it is safe and nothing hurts

Home is my breath and my pulse

White butterfly flickers by a pond, my ancestors
send a message from you.
Do my dreams reach?

Still looking

LETTERS UNDER ROCK

Dear Wanderer,

These eternal cycles fall into love and hate,
will you follow me

until the end?

Time

Remember my name

Sacrifice
Before

The bones and flesh

An altar
Bodies

Ash

In the evening, I catch the gentle moonlight
and wait. Will your spirit grace me in morning

starlight?

All are but a speck of dust

Caught in a sunbeam

The soul goes on living,
and takes on a new body

If I come back as a blue butterfly
in your dreams, will you recognize my
sacredness?

Never-ending

HAUNTED | MIRAGE | CONSCIOUS | **RELEARN**

Dear Nomad,

        I am new body. Now bird.
That day I become a heron. My white wings
spread
grace, calm, and tranquility.
Creator of light, I walk a carpet of clouds
toward the sun.
I land with one foot
on Earth, one in shallow
water. I wait to hunt.

I miss my spiders.
I don't know what to think of you.

Resurrect the memory of a sparrow nesting
in one hand and you hold loose the other.
I was an orphan with love letters
glued to my skin.
Vines wrapped my oak leaves dress.

What remains: The idea of your smile,
a lie about staying
here, a raven's wing we preserved in cornmeal.

Vacate my body,
capture the beginning again.

Dear Wanderer,

Storm clouds gather the heavens,
form a small planet with smoky
black and white scales.
                    The divine dragon appears
over its surface. Born of the calm without beginning
or
end, I float beyond sleep.

                    Awaken phoenix
                    meteor falls to earth, red
lightning.

Still you choose me on the path
to incarnation, a sparkling koi
swimming upstream until perfection.
You, a snowy egret, dance along frozen
ponds, raising crow feathers.

A clear night
sky above an ocean made of glass.
The harp quiets.

Epilogue

Don't be satisfied with stories, how things have gone with others. Unfold your own myth.
— Rumi

What matters is how well you walk through the fire.
— Charles Bukowski

Reflection

Dear Dragon,

My reflection shines swift
across the sea. A greater world
beyond

this world. A single feather
connects our souls
in the divine realm. Rouses
feelings about you,
not thoughts

Another

Dear Phoenix,

My heart shines
against the drift of time.
Use both hands to embrace
the sky as rain washes regret
without bitterness.

The tragedy of dreams imprisoned,
but love lets me go, and life
releases the world of another moon.
I glimpse snowfall
and smile as you appear
again

About the Authors

Cindy Rinne creates art and writes in San Bernardino, CA. She is Poet in Residence for the Neutra Institute Gallery and Museum, Los Angeles, CA. A Pushcart nominee. Cindy is the author of several books: Letters Under Rock with Bory Thach (Elyssar Press), Mapless with Nikia Chaney (Cholla Needles Press), Moon of Many Petals (Cholla Needles Press), Listen to the Codex (Yak Press), and others. A finalist for the 2016 Hillary Gravendyk Prize. Her poetry appeared or is forthcoming in: Anti-Herion Chic, Unpsychology Magazine, Foliate Oak Literary Magazine, MORIA, The Halcyone Literary Review, Verse of Silence, several anthologies, and others. www.fiberverse.com

Bory Thach was born in a refugee camp located on the border between Thailand and Cambodia. His family immigrated to the United States when he was four years old. He served in the U.S. Army and deployed to Iraq in support of Operation Iraqi Freedom. He has an MFA from California State University San Bernardino. Fiction and creative nonfiction fall under the art of storytelling, while poetry for him is more of a study of language, an art form in itself. His work appeared or is forthcoming in: Pacific Review, Urban Ivy, Arteidolia, and Sand Canyon Review.

About the Photographer

Edwin Vasquez is a prolific, multifaceted artist, who has developed a unique visual language. He offers the Antelope Valley a breath of fresh air with his photography, poetry, and vibrant mixed-media work. Vasquez's work is fearless in its social commentary, using rich forms and colors to provoke passionate responses to his ideas around the environment, waste and human nature. Edwin is an Artist in Residence at MOAH in Lancaster, CA until 2020 and attends Kipaipai, Professional Development Workshops which are part of AC Projects. Also, he is a photojournalist, published author, and videographer. He was born in Quetzaltenango, Guatemala in 1964.

Acknowledgments

Grateful to the following literary magazines in which these poems first appeared, some in a slightly different form:

Anti-Heroin Chic: "The Silence of Being" and "No Address"

Cholla Needles Arts & Library: "Ganesh admires branches reaching towards rebirth"

Cloud Women's Quarterly: "Wilderness," "Lunar Halo," and "Mirage"

Foliate Oak Literary Magazine: "Rewritten Story"

Harbor Review: "Ancestors are Here"

Picaroon Poetry: "Womb"

Poppy Road Review: "Sage Skull" and "Break the Surface Tension"

swifts and slows (Arteidolia): "Rebirth," "Yin and Yang," and "Conscious Presence"

The Halcyone Literary Review, Sixty Four Best Poets of 2018: "Under New Moon" and "Absence"

Unpsychology Magazine: "Sonic Air," "Hush," "Absence of Shadows," and "As in a Mirror"

Urban Ivy, Love You Anthology: "Thin Air" and "Vibrations"

Verse of Silence: "Silken"

Clothes for the performance were sewn by Cindy Rinne.

Thank you to John Brantingham who gave input on the first poems which became the performance. To Pauline Dutton who asked the right questions. Big thank you to Kelly Dortch for endless hours of line-by-line edits and discussion which made the letters go deeper. To Dorothy M. Barresi, M.F.A. for input on "Ganesh." Suzanne Lummis who challenged us to create worlds.

Thank you to Edwin Vasquez for his amazing photographs at MOAH (Museum of Art & History, Lancaster, CA), and to Andi Campognone, Director at MOAH for hosting our poetry performance during the "Woven Stories" exhibition.

Thank you to Katia Aoun Hage and Elyssar Press for the idea to create a performance poetry book and for believing in us.

Notes

Air, After Michael Brewster

Celebrate the boundary
Where streams join the sea,
Where body meets infinity.
"The Radiance Sutras," #44
Lorin Roche

Sage, The Sage speaks
for forty years
without saying a word.
Ramesh Chaitanya Balsekar

Map, Map the places that live in your memory
Map the voices of the land
"Counter Mapping" by Adam Loften
& Emmanuel Vaughan-Lee,
syndicated from emergencemagazine.org

Love is a naked shadow on a gnarled and naked tree.
Langston Hughes
"Song for a Dark Girl" from "Fine Clothes to the Jew," 1927

The highest of goodness is like water,
for water is excellent in benefitting all things.
Lionel Giles trans., "The Sayings of Lao Tzu."

Who is the Buddha?
The mountains are traveling over the sea.
Zen Buddhism, A Peter Pauper Press Book

Gaze, After Natalie J. Graham

Haunted, after Dulce Stein

Love alone is the fountain from which all virtues fall
as drops of sparkling water.
Bowl of Saki, October 8, by Hazrat Inayat Khan

Relearn, after Nancy Youdelman

www.ingramcontent.com/pod-product-compliance
Lightning Source LLC
Chambersburg PA
CBHW061211070526
44583CB00025B/3201